Children, Can You Hear Me?

How to Hear and See God

Written by Brad Jersak
Illustrated by Ken Save

Cover and interior art: Ken Save - contact him at kdsave@shaw.ca
Editorial direction: Kevin Miller - contact him at www.kevinwrites.com
Children's Bible paraphrase: Brad Jersak

Printed in Canada by Friesens
Produced in Europe via www.createspace.com

National Library of Canada Cataloguing in Publication
Jersak, Brad, 1964–
Children, Can You Hear Me? / Brad Jersak.

Fresh Wind **ISBN 978-0-9780174-7-7**
Create Space ISBN 978-1490405773

1. Spiritual life–Christianity–Juvenile literature.
2. Prayer–Christianity–Juvenile literature. I. Title.
BV212.J37 2003   248.8'2   C2003-911120-2

Fresh Wind Press
2170 Maywood Ct.,
Abbotsford, BC
CANADA V2S 4Z1
Web site: www.freshwindpress.com
E-mail: freshwind@shaw.ca

Children, Can You Hear Me?

How to Hear and See God

Written by Brad Jersak
Illustrated by Ken Save

Fresh Wind Press

For Stephen, Justice, and Dominic

Jesus said, "Let the little children come to me. Don't get in their way, because the kingdom of heaven belongs to people just like them."

- Matthew 19:14

How to use this book

Once, the disciples asked Jesus, "Who is the greatest person in God's kingdom?" Jesus called a little child to stand with him. Then he said, "Unless you change and become like little children, you can't even get into the kingdom of heaven. And you sure won't be the greatest one there until you're as humble as this child. When you welcome children like this, you are welcoming me."

—Matthew 18:1–5

Recently, my six-year old son Dominic took a copy of my first book—*Can You Hear Me? Tuning in to the God who speaks*—to school. Although the book was written for adults, Dominic read the first page to his class for show and tell. Shortly after that, he invited me out for a special lunch date, during which he informed me that it was time for me to write a children's version of the book. By noon the next day, two different adults approached me independently with the same request. Herein is my response.

You can use this book with children in a variety of ways. To begin with, you can read it through with them quite easily in a single sitting. But you'll also notice that each page can act as a stand-alone, daily children's devotional accompanied by a paraphrased Scripture. After reading the book straight through a couple of times, you may want to read it through again, this time pausing at each page to discuss the point it raises. Encourage children to ask questions of both you and God.

Most pages are also suitable as "listening prayer" exercises. For example, one page deals with meeting God in your best memory. To turn this into a listening prayer exercise, have children close their eyes and recall everything they can about a favorite memory, including sights, sounds, smells, and tastes. Once they have painted the full mental picture, have the children search for Jesus in that picture and then tell you what he is doing or saying. Invite them to approach him and interact with him as a friend.

My wife Eden and I have used each of these exercises many times with our own children. God continues to answer in fresh ways and has developed a growing friendship with each of our three boys. They've learned to recognize the tone of God's voice just as one recognizes the voice of a close friend.

Finally, I've also written this book for the little boy or girl inside of you—the one who needs to overhear what Jesus is saying to his children. Regardless of your age, if you are able to hear this message as an eager and willing child, take heart! You might just be entering the kingdom of heaven!

. . . .

Children, can you hear me?

Of course you can!
Just call on me, and I will answer you.
Some call me God or Lord.
Others call me Jesus. What do you call me?

You can call on me by praying.
Praying is talking to me
just like you talk to your friends.
When you talk to me, I hear you and answer you.
I come to you and show myself to you.

It's kind of like show and tell.

Whenever you call on me, I will answer you, and I will show you
great and wonderful things that will surprise you!

—Jeremiah 33:3

You won't usually hear me with your ears
or *see me with your eyes*—
although I might surprise you...

But your heart will *see* me,
your heart will *hear* me,
and your heart will *know* me.

That's because I made you!

Jesus said, "My Father loves anyone who loves me. I love you too,
and I will show myself to you."

—John 14:21

I pray that the eyes of your heart would be open and bright. Then
you will see the free gifts God has planned to give you. They are rich
and glorious, and they belong to you.

—Ephesians 1:18

Your heart can hear my voice.
What does it sound like to you?

Sometimes my voice is quiet and gentle
like a wind whispering through the trees.
Listen closely... Can you hear it?

Sometimes it's loud and strong
like thunder on a stormy night.
Don't be frightened; I'm just that big.

I speak in many different ways
so you can hear me in a way that's just right for you.

What does my voice sound like right now?

God really does speak, sometimes one way, sometimes another,
even when you might not be listening.

—Job 33:14

Your heart can see my face.
What does it look like to you?
What expression do you see?

When you look at my face,
You will see how much I love you.
You will see that I care about how you are doing.
You will see that I enjoy your company.

Sometimes I look happy. Ask me why!
One reason is because I think you're terrific,
and I'm glad to be your friend.

Sometimes I look sad. Ask me why.
Maybe I'm sad because I know you are sad.
But we can cheer each other up!

Show me your face; let me hear your voice.
Because your voice is sweet and your face is full of love.

—Song of Solomon 2:14

My face is usually cheerful and gentle.
It is never nervous or afraid.
That's because I'm strong and confident!

My face isn't mean or scary… at least not to you.

But if evil comes to hurt you, then I can get angry.
Don't be afraid. Just ask me to take care of it.
After all, love takes care of people, doesn't it?

Keep looking at Jesus with the eyes of your heart. He opened them
up to begin with, and he'll help you to see him perfectly some day.

—Hebrews 12:2

When you pray, you aren't just talking to me.
We're talking to each other.
We're hanging out
Just like you hang out with your friends.

I love hanging out with you!

Come close and talk to me.
I'm the best listener ever.
Tell me about your day.
What made you happy?
What made you sad?
How about a hug?

Jesus said, "Instead of being my servant, I'd like you to be my friend.
Servants don't get to hear secrets, but friends do. So I'll call you my
friend, because I tell you everything my Father tells me."

—John 15:15

We can hang out anywhere,
because I'm always with you.
You can meet me in all your favorite places.

Want to meet me in your bedroom?
I'm there. Can you see me?
Remember to use your heart-eyes!
What am I doing? What am I saying?
I'll stay there with you and keep you company.

Do you have a favorite hiding place?
I'll meet you there too.
We can sit together and just be quiet—
or we can make secret plans for the day!

God, you're always ahead of me, leading the way. But you're also
behind me, following along. You're always close enough to hold my
hand. That's so amazing—I can hardly believe it.

—Psalm 139:5–6

When you go out, I go with you.
I'm always tagging along.
Do you go to the park? You'll find me there.
How about school? I'm there, too.
Church? Yes, even there.

I have a place I love to go.
Would you like to come?
Just close your eyes...

Wherever I go, I always find you.
And when I run away, you always find me. If I went as high as heaven,
you'd be there. If I looked deep in the earth, you'd be there too.
What if I could fly to the place where the sun comes up? What if I
could swim to the bottom of the ocean? Yes, your hand would still
be holding me safe and showing me the way.

—Psalm 139:7-10

Meet me in your imagination.
Your imagination is a place where your heart
can create just about anything!
I gave you your imagination.
Do you like it?

You can use your imagination to think about
good things or bad things.
But I gave it to you so we could meet there together.

If you could build any place with your imagination,
what would it look like?
Wow, I like it! I'll meet you there.

God can even do more than you ask or imagine, because his power,
that no one can measure, is working inside of you.

—Ephesians 3:20

One of my favorite places is your heart.
Can you believe that?
Your heart is where I live.
I've made it my special home.

Close your eyes, what does your heart-place look like?
Some people see a sturdy castle.
Others see a cozy cabin or a fancy playhouse.
What do you see?

Can you see me there?
What am I doing? What am I saying?
What shall we do? What shall we play?

God is my fortress. I hide in him to keep safe.

—Psalm 94:22

Another favorite place of mine is my throne room.
See my throne? What does it look like?
See me sitting there? What am I wearing?

Look! I have such a big lap!
Come on up and sit for a while.
The world looks interesting from here.

Wow, look at all those people!
And how about all those angels!

Lean your ear against my chest.
Can you hear my heart beating?
It's beating with love for you.

When I prayed, I saw a throne in heaven,
and someone was sitting on it.

—Revelation 4:2

Do you remember my cross?
You can meet me there, too.
Do you *see* me?

My cross is a good place to leave your burdens.
A burden is anything that makes you feel bad.
What makes you feel bad?
Would you like to leave it here with me?

I'll take all of your burdens, if you like.
They're much easier for me to carry.
No problem at all.

Can I have them?

Let God carry everything and everyone that you care about,
because he cares about you.

—1 Peter 5:7

We can also meet in a big grassy field
or beside a gurgling creek.
I am a Good Shepherd,
and you are one of my lambs.
We can rest there together or we can play.

What do you want to do?
Do you want to lie in the grass and look at the clouds?
Should we chase each other around the field?
Maybe we can splash around in the stream.
Your choice.

God takes care of us like a shepherd. He gathers each lamb in his
arms and carries them close to his heart.

—Isaiah 40:11

How about meeting me in a garden?
I love gardens. That's where life began.

What kind of plants do you see?
Look at the sun shining through the leaves!
What color are the flowers? How do they smell?
How about the fruit? Go ahead and pick one.
What does it taste like?

Can you find me among the trees?
Come, let's play hide and seek together!
It's one of my favorite games.
If you seek me, you'll soon find me.
I'll make sure of that. I promise.

God's children will be like a freshly rained on garden. They won't be
unhappy ever again. The girls will dance and be glad. The boys will
join in too. Even the old people will take a turn.
I will turn their tears into laughter.

—Jeremiah 31:13

We can also meet in just about any Bible story.
Which one is your favorite?
Daniel and the lion's den?
Jonah and the whale?
David and Goliath?
How about when I was walking on the water?
Can you see the story in your heart?

Try stepping into a story.
Can you find me there?
What am I doing? What am I saying?
Where are you in the story?
Are you one of the characters?
Come close and talk to me.
We'll live the story together.

I keep your word in the hiding place of my heart.

—Psalm 119:11

I can meet you in your memories.
What's your very best memory?
Can you see it with your heart?
I was there. Can you find me?
What am I doing? What am I saying?

What's your very worst memory?
How did you feel?
I was there, too. Can you find me?
What am I doing? What am I saying?

You can run to me.
Tell me the whole story. Ask me to help.
I'll take those burdens, too.

God always walks in front of you and goes wherever you go.
He will never leave you or stop being your friend.
With him around, fear and sadness soon leave.

—Deuteronomy 31:8

I can also meet you in your dreams.
Do you remember any of your dreams?
You can step back into your dreams
even when you're awake.
If you pick one, you can find me there.

Have a look around.
What am I doing?
Watch and listen.
You may be surprised.

I had a dream about a stairway from earth all the way to heaven.
The angels were climbing up and down,
and God was standing at the top.

—Genesis 28:12–13

I have good news for you:
I can even meet you in your nightmares.
If you wake up at night from a scary dream,
just call me, and I will answer you.
You won't be afraid of the dark
if you remember it's just my shadow.

Do you remember any of your nightmares?
What are they about?

Try to find me there. I'll help if you like.
Watch what I do.

I love to rescue people.

If you live in God's shelter, you'll be able to rest quietly in his shadow.
You won't have to be afraid of scary nighttime things.

—Psalm 91:1, 5

Whenever you see me; that's called faith.
Faith is seeing what I show your heart.
Faith is hearing what I say to your heart.
Faith is believing whatever I show you or tell you
Even before it happens, because I always tell the truth.

Faith helps you hear me and see me better and better.
Is it getting easier for you to hear and see me now?

Faith is seeing what you hope for with your heart
and knowing it's going to happen.

—Hebrews 11:1

When we meet, how can you know it's really me?
That's easy!

If you hear and see things that make you
hate others or yourself,
That's not me.

If you hear and see things that make you
feel afraid or ashamed,
That's not me either.

And if you hear and see things that make you
want to hide from me,
You guessed it: Not me.

There's no one quite like me!

Keep listening to God. Don't think that what you're hearing is silly.
But listen carefully and only hang on to the good stuff.
You can throw the rest away.

—1 Thessalonians 5:19–22

The things I say are right and true and pure.
They help you to love me and other people.
They also help you lift others up when they feel low.
Or stand up for them when no one else will.
They give you strength and comfort, joy, and peace.

Another way to be sure it's me
is to compare what you hear in your heart with
how I sound in my book, the Bible
or with what I say to other people who know me.

If you're not sure it's me, just ask!

The things God says are always pure. He tells us to love peace and
to be gentle all the time. God tells us how to agree with others,
how to be kind to them, and how to do good things for them.
He shows us how to be fair and honest with everyone.

—James 3:17

Remember: I am your friend,
so you can ask me anything.

Here are some questions you can ask me:

What excites you these days? Why?
What makes you sad these days? Why?

When was the last time you laughed with me? Why?
When was the last time you cried for me? Why?

What do you like best about me?
What do you see when you look at me?

When we meet in heaven,
what is the first thing you will say to me?
I can hardly wait to tell you!

God is a friend who sticks closer than a brother.

—Proverbs 18:24

I enjoyed hanging out with you.
Thanks for taking the time to listen
and to share your heart with me.

Remember: We can do this anytime, anywhere.
Just open your heart's eyes and ears, and I'll be there.
We'll hang out, because that's what friends do.

Thank you for being my friend!

The friends of Jesus wait and listen for him.
And they are full of joy when they hear his voice.

—John 3:29

Listening Prayer
With Children

Secret things belong to God, but the things he shares will always belong to us and our kids, so that we can obey everything he's asked us to do.

                   - Deuteronomy 29:29

Jesus said, "I praise you, Father, Ruler of heaven and earth, because you have hidden your secrets from people who think they know so much, but you whispered them to little children. Why, Father? Just because it made you happy!"

                   - Matthew 11:25–26

Jesus called a little child and had him stand right there. He said: "This is true: unless you become like little children, you won't ever enter the kingdom of heaven."

                   - Matthew 18:2–3

RUINED GARDENS

My son Dominic, who was four years old at the time, crawled onto my lap and leaned in close. We were sitting in the front row of a Bible College chapel. I had been teaching there for orientation week and was about to share my final "two cents worth." As the worship time wound down, I asked Domo, "What is God showing you about the students here?" He briefly scanned the crowd over my shoulder and replied, "God is telling me that some of them have ruined gardens." The imagery stunned me. In Song of Solomon, the garden is a specific symbol for a woman's sexuality (Song of Solomon 4:12—5:1). In that context, a locked garden represents the bride's virginity. Her invitation to the lover to enter her garden and taste its fruit is a picture of consensual intercourse. Of course, Domo knew none of this. Yet to me, the image of the ruined garden (i.e., sexual brokenness) was so striking that I followed it up, "What does Jesus want to do about that?" He replied, "Jesus wants to plant new flowers in their gardens." This spoke to me of restored innocence. At the end of my message, I related Dominic's message, but refrained from interpreting it for the students. Afterwards, several of the young women approached my wife and me, confessing through their tears that the picture was about them. It was the Father's good pleasure to reveal his word to a hidden issue through the mouth of a child.

A Parent's Job

Scripture teaches that parents are responsible to lead their children into an intimate friendship with God. More than anyone else, mom and dad must teach their children that God speaks to them.

> Only be careful, and watch yourselves closely so that you do not forget the things your eyes have seen or let them slip from your heart as long as you live. Teach them to your children and to their children after them. (Deuteronomy 4:9 NIV)

> Fix these words of mine in your hearts and minds; tie them as symbols on your hands and bind them on your foreheads. Teach them to your children, talking about them when you sit at home and when you walk along the road, when you lie down and when you get up. (Deuteronomy 11:18-19 NIV)

Children hear the Lord easier than anyone else. Virtually the only block that I encounter in them is their parents' own unbelief. If we will assume, as children often do, that God is *already* speaking to them, we can nurture their ability to tune in to his voice.

I woke up to this truth when my friend Phil heard his five-year-old son Richard talking to an adult male in his bedroom. Alarmed by the voice, Phil ducked into the room to see who it was that invaded their home. Richard stood there alone.

Phil looked around the room, "Who was that I heard talking to you in here?"

"God," Richard replied, as if this were normal.

Here's my point: It *is* normal. Children who *can't* hear the Lord anymore (yes, *anymore*) have usually been inadvertently shut down by an adult.

In this chapter, I hope to equip you with creative spiritual exercises and suggestions that will help you maintain and develop a "hearing heart" in your children whether they're at home, at church or another ministry setting.

1. Assume your child already hears God.

The earlier you expect your child to sense God's presence and voice, the less likely you are to shut down their spiritual eyes and ears. Remember that they will be using their imaginations (which can be pretty wild to adult ears), but that is the venue they are providing for Jesus to come. And he will. My niece Cassie meets with Jesus on a giant imaginary lollypop. Dominic meets him in a mental petting zoo. Your initial skepticism will begin to melt as you hear the profound and intimate conversations that ensue.

To begin with, you might try stating a Scripture truth and then asking your child a follow-up question. For example,

- God is in the room with us right now. Where do you see him? What's he doing? What's he look like? (Assume in faith that they know).
- God talks to us all the time. What is he telling you? What is he showing you? How is he feeling now?
- You may need to explain that even if they don't see him or hear him with their eyes or ears, they *can* see him and hear him with their hearts. So what's he doing? What's he saying in your heart?

2. Invite your child to find Jesus in a meeting place.

I hope that you are convinced of the reality and necessity of treating prayer as a real meeting with a living Friend. I believe that every child can and should be trained to know Jesus as their best friend and to meet with him in a variety of meeting venues.

Again, assume in faith that Jesus will meet your child (and probably has already). Don't make that the issue. Start with the truth that he wants to meet them. The question is "where?" The answer: "Anywhere that they can imagine." Here are some questions to get you started:

- Jesus lives in your heart. What does it look like? If he could meet you anywhere at all, what would that place look like? What's he doing there? (Hint: It's wonderful to have the child draw or paint that place.)
- Jesus is with you in the house, the bedroom, the backyard, at school, everywhere. Where is he right now? What's he up to? What's he saying?
- Jesus meets us at church. Where is he? What's he doing? Are there any angels here today (very common)? (Hint: Let them draw what they imagine is happening during the worship.)

- Jesus wants to meet you in your favourite Bible story. Which one? Where is he? What's he doing? What's he saying? Teach your child how to "step into" Bible stories through his or her imagination.

Our second son, Justice, loves to ask, "Dad, can we do one of those Bible stories where we go into the story?" His favourite is when Jesus was asleep in the fishing boat. As I read or tell Justice the story, I pause after each sentence to ask him to describe what he is seeing. For example, "Jesus and his disciples were out at sea when a storm came up. Justice, can you see the boat? What does it look like? What does the sea look like? Tell me about the storm. What are the disciples doing?" Invariably, Justice decides that he had better go wake Jesus up. He finds him sleeping, wakes him up, and watches him calm the storm. Here's the catch: Then we ask Jesus if there is anything else he would like to tell Justice. Consistently, Justice will see and hear the Lord speaking out promises and blessings in a flood of very pure revelation. It is so precious to hear the heart of the Lord for our sons every time we practice this.

◀)) Tuning In

If you have or relate to any children, try a "stepping in" exercise with them. Ask them to choose the Bible story. Then in each case, invite the child to find Jesus, approach him, touch him, talk to him, and listen to him. This is not merely a movie for them to watch. It's a real meeting in which they participate. You might be surprised at the beautiful truths that surface.

3. Convert bedtime prayers into listening prayers.

Most parents are used to walking their children through some standard prayers at bedtime. It's not difficult to convert these rituals into three-way conversational prayers between you, your child, and Jesus. You can ask the question, the Lord can provide the answer to your child, and your child can report it back to you. This format can become a natural pattern for family prayer. Here are some starter questions you may want to try:

- Jesus, is there anything today that we could thank you for? Why?
- Is there anything that we need to say sorry for? Will you forgive me?
- Is there anyone you want us to pray for? How? (Family, friend, and missionary photo albums are terrific for this. So are atlases or missions handbooks that give children a global vision.)
- Are there any *burdens* we are carrying that you want to lift for us? If so, ask Jesus where the burden came from, what it is, and if he would please remove it.

- Jesus, do you have any *promises or blessings* for me before I go to sleep?
- Bonus question: Jesus, what was the best part of *your* day? What made *you* happy?

For years, my son Stephen was an insomniac. By the time he was eight, he was able to ruin a good night's sleep by mulling over worries with the best of them. He would commonly lie awake in bed for several hours before settling down to sleep. But on the same weekend that he had his visitation from the Lord, he started falling asleep within ten minutes. We asked his secret. He said that he had devised a scheme in which he gathers up all the day's problems in prayer and jams them into one little knapsack. Then he walks to the cross, finds Jesus there, and offers him the knapsack. The Lord places it on the ground and sets it on fire. The image of the living Christ by the cross is the resting place for Stephen's anxiety and his weary head.

4. Invite Jesus into nightmares and night terrors.

Children seem to be born with their spiritual windows wide open. You don't have to look far to hear angel-stories from very young children. Our second son Justice has periodically seen angels in our house, outside in the trees, and running beside our car. Of course, children also commonly complain about "monsters" in their bedroom at night. Night terrors, nightmares, monsters under the bed or in the closet, when not a dietary or health-related issue, can often be explained as:

- Actual spiritual oppression
- Imaginary projections from real fears
- Annoying bedtime stalling tactics

In many cases, a child's own fears activate their imagination in order to delay their bedtime. Rather than rebuking them for believing in something that is not real, I find it much more helpful to invite Jesus into the room to deal with the monsters. I ask the Lord to show our kids the angels and invite them to clean house. This is very important for two reasons.

First, if the monsters are really just a projection of the child's fears, why not flush the fear out rather than repress it? And who better to eradicate fear than the Lord Jesus, who is happy to use the child's imagination to bring about peace? He loves to train them to fear no evil by "practicing his presence."

Second, if the monsters are actually unclean spirits that the child perceives through his or her spiritual windows, then the "not real" message bears awful fruit. It ignores the child's real oppression, leaving them plagued with fear. Worse, it hamstrings them from seeing the Lord or his angels come to their aid.

Diane is just one of many of my friends who bore the wounds of this message throughout childhood. She began to see monsters in her bedroom at night in open-eyed visions during her pre-school years. When she reported it to her parents, they never introduced Jesus or the angels into the problem. Instead, they would either punish her or negate what she said. The message she heard was that what she was seeing was not real. They chalked it up to an "active imagination." She wondered if she was crazy and tried to pretend that the monsters weren't there. But she continued to see the evil images—*right into adulthood!* While the "not real" message could not deliver her from evil, it *did* create a blinding filter for good things. She now found it much easier and more common to see demonic spirits than to perceive the Lord. Prayer ministry has slowly rectified this malady. Only now in her thirties has she become aware of the presence of Jesus and his angels round about her.

In all of these cases, listening prayer is an appropriate and efficient way to resolve things. We don't deny what they are experiencing. We invite Jesus in. We ask him what the monsters are, where they came from, and what he wants to do about them. I'm not afraid to attach consequences if the trouble continues, but initially I threaten the monster, not the child. For example, "Jesus, can it come back? If it tries to come back, Jesus what will you do to it?" Then we speak a final truth over the child, "Jesus is here now and you can tuck him in with you. You're totally safe. Good night."

5. Take conflicts at school and at home to Jesus.

When our children have a rough day at school, we try to find out as soon as they get home. Whether they had trouble with the teacher or other students, we do a mini inner healing with them. The same goes for when they experience conflicts at home with their siblings or with Eden and me as parents. We come before the Lord together, finding him in the situation and meeting him at the cross.

- What happened? How did that make you feel? Why?
- Where was Jesus when that happened? What was he doing or saying?
- Would you like Jesus to lift away the hurt and anger?
- Ask Jesus to show you the others through his eyes. Can you send these people to the cross and leave them there?
- Is there anything you need to say sorry for?
- Does Jesus have a promise for you about this?

6. Help your children interpret their dreams.

We enjoy listening to each other's dreams in the morning. Often the kids will wake us up and sit on the bed, describing their night time escapades. These morning dreams are fun to interpret with Jesus' help. We invite him to identify the symbols in the dream and the message that he has for us that day. Asking Jesus what each object and person represents keeps us in an intuitive ("right brain") space. This type of interpretation flows much more easily than shifting into analytical dream-dictionary modes. Assume that the children will hear Jesus' interpretation without even having to think through it. The very first thought that comes to their minds when we ask Jesus a question is usually right on.

7. Incorporate listening prayer into Sunday school.

We use listening prayer in every Sunday school class at Fresh Wind. Every child is taught how to find a meeting place with Jesus, how to step into a Bible story, and is given two to three questions to ask Jesus when they get there. The children who are teaching our Sunday school classes have a lesson-planning outline that makes preparation a listening prayer exercise. Here's how it looks:

- Read the passage. Ask Jesus to highlight the verses he wants to emphasize. Ask Jesus, "What's the main point of this story?"
- Learn the story well enough to help the class step into the story.
- Ask Jesus to show you a time when you saw this main point happen in your life. Where was Jesus in that event? What was he doing?
- Ask God for questions that the class can ask him together.

Regardless of the topic, each week the children practice their skills in hearing, obeying, and acting on God's voice.

My son Stephen used the above lesson plan to teach the kindergarten to grade three class the story of Jesus and the ten lepers. When he read the story, God highlighted the importance of thanksgiving when asking for healing prayer. However, by the time we arrived at church, Stephen was in tears with a severe headache and ready to bail out of teaching. During pre-service prayer, we prayed for him while he focused only on thanksgiving and praise (practicing what he was going to teach). After two or three minutes of prayer, he testified that his pain had gone from a "10" to a "7." He went into the service and continued in praise for two songs, then received communion. The headache vanished completely.

After worship, Stephen went to class with a dramatically updated lesson illustration. He taught on the ten lepers, shared his experience and then brought his class into the main service. As my message wound down, the little band of intercessors roamed the room, asking Jesus who needed prayer for healing. They surrounded and soaked one person after another in prayer as God led them. No one will remember my message. But the image of children moving as one, hovering around the sick and disabled, will remain with us for a long time.

A Final Secret

As our congregation has practiced listening prayer with their children, true to his word Jesus is revealing the "hidden things" to our little children (Matthew 11:26). Only with childlike trust will we ever enter into those kingdom secrets. So here is my advice:

Your children hear God. If you wake up to it yourself, so will they. When they call on the Lord, he does answer them. For every page of revelation you read into your children's words, the Lord will write an entire journal's worth. When you learn to hear God's voice through them, the secrets of the kingdom are just around the corner. Why? Because the kingdom of heaven belongs to them. What is not received is not given. But to those who receive, "a little child will lead them" (Isaiah 11:6).

∙ ∙ ∙ ∙ ∙ ∙ ∙ ∙ ∙ ∙ ∙ ∙ ∙ ∙ ∙ ∙ ∙ ∙ ∙

Also available from Fresh Wind Press

Can You Hear Me? Tuning
In To The God Who Speaks.
by Brad Jersak

Can You Hear Me? is a combination
of biblical and historical research,
real life testimonies, and inspiring
exercises on listening prayer. God
desires to transform your prayers
into intimate conversations—real
meetings with a living Friend. You
will become aware that encountering
God is more simple, accessible, and
interactive than you ever dreamed.

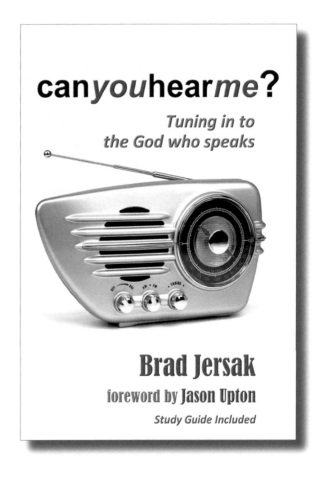

Brad Jersak

Brad is a bewildered dad with three unique boys and a lovely wife named Eden.
He grew up on the prairies beside Killarney Lake. Now he lives in Abbotsford, BC.
That's in Canada. He attends Fresh Wind, a fun little church with lots of children
and other child-like people. He loves teaching people how to hear and see God.

Made in United States
Troutdale, OR
10/02/2024

23219981R00040